Johnny Unitas
The Best There Ever Was

TRIUMPH
BOOKS
CHICAGO

Contributors

Photography
AP/Wide World Photo

Linc Wonham ... Editor
Ray Ramos ... Designer

This book is available in quantity at special discounts for your group or organization. For further information, contact:

Triumph Books
601 South LaSalle Street
Suite 500
Chicago, Illinois 60605
(312) 939-3330
Fax (312) 663-3557

Printed in the United States of America

ISBN: 1-57243-546-1

Contents

Chapter 1

The Golden Arm of a Golden Era

With a name like that he could have been president. And many Sunday afternoons it seemed like he was, with the way he played.

He had the perfect name for a quarterback. The job, of course, required much more than a name, especially if you were going to play well enough to make folks call you "the best there ever was."

More than a few of football's greats have been tagged with that line over the decades. But he was the one who lived up to it, who kept living up to it long after he played, even after the rules had been changed so that NFL defenses were no longer allowed a stranglehold on the passing game.

Stranglehold or no stranglehold, he shoved the issue right into the teeth of the defense every time he stepped on the field. The unassuming specter of Mr. Colt—the black, high-topped shoes, the sloped shoulders, the crew cut, the seamless technique, the unshakeable demeanor—lorded over the game with an impenetrable cool. And he had that name.

"Unite us."

With a name like that he could have been president. And many Sunday afternoons it seemed like he was, with the way that he played.

"He had so much courage," said the wife of one of his offensive linemen, the awe still obvious in her voice decades after John Constantine Unitas played his last NFL game. That courage evidenced itself virtually every fall Sunday afternoon for 18 seasons. He played in an age of unrestrained defenses, when pass rushers were allowed to wield the head slap on blockers, then move on to sack the quarterback with little fear of roughing-the-passer rules.

Head coach Weeb Ewbank briefs Unitas (No. 19) and the rest of the Colts for the next day's 1958 title game against the New York Giants at Yankee Stadium in New York.

Meanwhile, downfield defensive backs could shove and push and generally assault receivers trying to run patterns. "The five-yard bump rule? . . . Hell, you and I could get open," Unitas once told *Sports Illustrated*'s Paul Zimmerman when asked about the modern game. "Liberalized pass-blocking rules? . . . A bunch of big fat guys just grabbing on."

"It was a completely different game back then," Hall of Famer Joe Montana said of the golden era that Unitas ruled. "Imagine if the receivers had free rein down the field like they do today—he might have set records that nobody would ever break."

He was the prototype of the drop-back passer, with a gambler's heart (although he always insisted he never gambled on any play, but simply exploited opponents' tendencies—which he had spent hours studying). One can only imagine his disdain if he had been forced to play in the modern, West Coast passing game.

Unitas lived to look upfield, to break defenders' hearts and spirits with a long strike. When he became the first pro QB to throw for 40,000 yards, it seemed no one could ever top that, or any of the other scores of passing records he set. But then the NFL went and changed the rules, simply because there were no other Johnny Us out there, no one fearless enough to step up and challenge defenses the way that he did.

"Sometimes I think he holds the ball an extra second," Merlin Olsen of the Rams' Fearless Foursome once told reporters. "Just to give you a shot at him, so he can show you he doesn't care."

He cared plenty—about winning—which is evidenced by his records and milestones, including:

• His selection as the "Greatest Player in the First 50 Years of Pro Football"
• His selection in 2000 as quarterback for the NFL's All-Time team by the panel of 36 Pro Football Hall of Fame voters
• His heroic role in the Colts' overtime win in the 1958 NFL championship, the "Greatest Game Ever Played"
• His numbers: 2,830 completed passes for 40,239 yards and a record 290 touchdown passes
• His unbreakable record of throwing TD passes in 47 consecutive games between 1956 and 1960
• His three seasons of 3,000 yards or more passing
• His selection as NFL player of the year in 1957, 1958, and 1964
• His inspiring leadership in directing the Colts to the 1958 and 1959 NFL championships
• His selection to 10 Pro Bowls
• His role as an aging performer in leading the Colts to the 1970 Super Bowl
• His retirement in 1973 with 22 NFL records, including most passes attempted and completed, most yards gained passing, most touchdown passes, and most seasons leading the league in TD passes
• His 1979 induction into the Pro Football Hall of Fame

"He is the greatest quarterback to ever play the game, better than I was, better than Baugh, better than anyone." —Sid Luckman

"Johnny Unitas is the greatest quarterback ever to play the game, better than I was, better than Sammy Baugh, better than anyone," Sid Luckman, the dominant Chicago Bears quarterback of the forties, once offered.

Unitas led a nation of baby boomers out of their childhood and adolescence toward their dreams. For Jeff Davis, a longtime sports television producer in Chicago and an author who is working on a biography of George Halas, the unforgettable Unitas moment came in November 1960 at Wrigley Field.

"The Bears and Colts were battling for the Western Division lead," Davis recalled. "The Bears were leading the Colts 20–17 with Baltimore driving at the end. They had halted the Colts at the 39, leaving them with fourth-and-long with about 40 seconds left after sacking Unitas.

"After a timeout the Colts opted against a field-goal attempt since [place-kicker] Steve Myhra was struggling. Unitas came out to shoot the works. He dropped back. Under Doug Atkins' pressure he threw long down the right side. The Bears defender, C. J. Caroline, matched Lenny Moore step for step.

"At the goal line, Moore pushed off and got away with it. Caroline fell down and Moore caught the touchdown in the end zone for a 24–20 Colts victory."

It was one of those defeats that Davis and millions of other Bears fans would never forget.

Just moments before making that big play, Unitas had been sitting on the sideline, his spirit seemingly crushed by the brutal Bears pass rush. There were cuts and scrapes on his cheeks, forehead, and nose. A trainer attended to him for a full five minutes while he gathered his wits and prepared to reenter the game.

Once he did he was able to assemble his teammates in the huddle for that one final play. Wrigley Field was already alive with the air of impending celebration. Then Unitas silenced it all with a pump fake and the 40-yard strike to Moore.

Sportswriters would later estimate that 3,000 fans waited outside Wrigley that day "just to revere him, to look at him," according to *Baltimore News-American* sportswriter John Steadman.

"The week after the monster mash in Chicago, the Colts played the Lions," Davis recalled. "Detroit was leading 9–8 with seconds to go when Unitas again hit Moore for the apparent winning touchdown. After they cleared the field of frenzied fans, Myhra converted to make it 15–9 Baltimore.

Moments before making that big play, Unitas had been sitting on the sideline with cuts and scrapes on his cheeks, forehead, and nose.

"Time remained for a kickoff and one play from scrimmage. From their 24 the Lions flooded the field with receivers against an eight-defensive-back set. Earl Morrall [then with the Lions] found the one open man—tight end Jim Gibbons—directly over the middle in between the coverage. Gibbons flew to the end zone for the 16–15 winner."

For Bears fans like Davis it was justice that "the cold-blooded efficiency of Johnny Unitas" had been repaid, if only for a moment.

The mark that Unitas left on a generation was indelible in a million different ways. For Patrick Flynn, an army colonel stationed in Florida, Unitas represented a memory of Flynn's father, who died too young.

One of Flynn's earliest and most vivid childhood memories is "watching a ballgame with my father and listening intently as he described in detail the way Unitas held the ball, deliberately dropped back into the pocket, and quickly delivered the ball with a perfect throwing motion. My dad described Unitas' actions as perfect, developed by Unitas through thousands and thousands of hours of practice in the pursuit of perfection. My dad was teaching me a lesson about persistence in the pursuit of excellence."

As he grew older, Flynn saw more of Unitas and learned a lesson about heart. "When he came into the game you *knew* there was a chance to win because you *knew* he was capable of greatness," he said.

For Frank Cooney, a senior editor at *USA Sports Weekly*, it was the experience of being a high school quarterback in San Francisco during Unitas' heyday that left its mark. "I liked to run," Cooney recalled, "so the then young and fast and already tough Billy Kilmer [out of UCLA and playing with the 49ers then] was somebody I watched. But his throwing motion was nothing you would want to copy. For that, myself and many young quarterbacks I knew looked to Johnny Unitas, whose grace as a passer was damn near an art form.

"Watching Johnny U's great throwing motion—over the top with that follow-through all the way to his hand being turned so his right pinky was pointing upward to the sky—it is a vision that was surely burned into the memories of those who were looking for a model, an example, some idea of what it took to be a good passer. That classic motion and his uncanny knack to throw to a spot where a receiver could go get the ball—it was a clinic and a precursor to the passing systems that were yet to come."

For Mike Ashley, a sportswriter who covers the Maryland Terrapins, the memory that stays with him is watching Unitas in the twilight

> "Johnny U's great throwing motion is a vision surely burned into the memories of those who were looking for a model, some idea of what it took to be a good passer."
> —Frank Cooney, *USA Sports Weekly*

of his career. "I remember the slow stroll to the line of scrimmage, the bowlegged gait as he surveyed the defense," Ashley recalled. "I remember the hunched shoulders and long arms, the quick, somehow smoothly frantic drop back, and that picture-book release. Unitas was still wearing a crew cut and black high-top cleats when I became a fan. He was still winning games too, except for his last season in Baltimore when the organization fell into so much disarray that they actually sold a legend to the San Diego Chargers.

"What I think of most when I think of Unitas, though, is my oldest brother," Ashley continued. "He came of age as a football fan in the fifties. It was his passion for the game and for Unitas that triggered my interest. I remember him giving me a 1971 pocket schedule booklet sponsored by some beer distributor. It had NFL schedules and rosters and statistics and I memorized most of it, including the three-deep for every team.

"Unitas led the Colts to the AFC Championship Game that winter only to have the upstart Miami Dolphins shut them out and go on to the Super Bowl, only to lose to Dallas. My brother didn't take that game as hard as I thought he would. He had already packed away so many great memories from the guy with the 'golden arm' that one setback couldn't diminish any of them.

"I used to love to hear those stories, like when Hall of Fame tight end John Mackey described being in the huddle with Unitas as like 'being in the huddle with God.' Or when

Ewbank (from left), Unitas, and backup QB George Shaw in 1958.

Unitas crossed up the vaunted New York Giants defense in the 'Greatest Game Ever Played,' the 1958 NFL championship, with a pass deep in Giants territory. Questioned by a reporter about the risk of interception, Unitas replied, 'When you know what you're doing, you don't get intercepted.'

"And there were times," Ashley said, "as I became older and it seemed my brother and I were worlds apart on so many issues, that football and family were the only conduits that linked us. Developing my own passion for sports, I still heard the childlike awe when he talked of things he'd seen Unitas do, and the thrills the Colts of the fifties and sixties brought to him, to a whole generation. . . . Those who saw Johnny U in his prime—and later saw Namath and Staubach and Montana and Marino and Elway—still put Unitas atop their lists. And that's something my brother and I can still agree on."

New England Patriots coach Bill Belichick is another fan from that generation. He grew up in Maryland while Unitas worked his magic. "Growing up in that area, every kid wanted to be Johnny Unitas," Belichick said.

It was an adulation well deserved, according to Raymond Berry, who as a Colts wide receiver was one

> "His mechanics were magnificent. He was the textbook: This is the way to drop back. This is the way to set up. This is the way to hold your elbows in. . . ." —Marv Levy

of Unitas' hard targets. "I will acknowledge other great quarterbacks and people are entitled to their opinions; I'll put Unitas' name in the hat and let them put in their choices," Berry said. "But I'll pick John as the greatest of all time. He was a rare combination of tangibles and intangibles. He had the physique, the tremendously strong arm, and he could hit the strike zone with every kind of pitch. He had such great leadership, and I think that's so significant. His object was to win the game. As a quarterback, it was his job to move the offense and score. He couldn't care less who did it. That attitude set the tone.

"As a passer, there was no throw he couldn't make," Berry added. "Plus he was so accurate. He could put the ball in places that were safe."

"His mechanics were magnificent," Hall of Fame coach Marv Levy agreed. "He was the textbook: This is the way to drop back. This is the way to set up. This is the way to direct your eyes and head down the field. This is the way to hold your elbows in. His mechanics were unparalleled. The closest I've ever seen to his mechanics is Peyton Manning."

Unitas offered a stealth that befuddled defenders, Berry said. "You couldn't tell anything from his eyes—only that his eyes were there."

Hall of Fame linebacker Sam Huff revealed that once he called nine different defenses in a New York Giants huddle during a game, only to have Unitas outsmart all nine looks.

"I always felt that he invented the two-minute drill," Hall of Famer Don Shula, who coached Unitas, recalled. "He seemed to have a clock in his head and always knew how much time he had to work with."

"No lead was safe if you were playing against Johnny," recalled Earl Morrall, a one-time teammate and former Colts QB, "and no game was out of reach if you were on his team."

"You'd knock him down," said longtime NFL defensive coach Bill Arnsparger, "but I'll be darned, he'd throw a touchdown pass to Raymond Berry or to Jimmy Orr or [John] Mackey or somebody. He'd always find a way to make it happen."

"There was a coolness and a constant 'in-control-of-the-situation, I-understand-what's-happening,' " Levy said. "There was never any sense of panic setting in, even in the most dire of situations. In order to make all of that work with a lot of great teammates around him, he had the magnificent balance between confidence and lack of ego. He's one of those guys who expected to succeed, but had no swagger."

"If you had to pick one guy, somebody who has to be the best, in my opinion he's the best," offered Ron Wolf, the former Green Bay Packers GM credited with finding and developing Brett Favre.

Wolf grew up in Pennsylvania near the Maryland state line and recalled taking leave from the army in 1957 to see Unitas work in Colts training camp. "I watched practice," Wolf told the *Baltimore Sun*. "And when Unitas was under center, it was obvious who the best one was. Unitas took command. He had that presence. Those people who do that have that presence."

"It's hard to imagine Unitas with a headset in his helmet, some coach feeding him information and the next play," sportswriter Ashley said. "Johnny U called his own plays and carried the fortunes of a team and a blue-collar, Colts-blue-clad town on those hunched shoulders. Of course, another part of his legacy is how little emotion Unitas ever showed on the field. He approached the game like a job to be done. Outcomes good or bad, he was a stoic expecting the same from his teammates, demanding their best and, like all great athletes, often willing them to efforts they didn't even know they were capable of.

"I remember a game late in his career when he led the Colts to a win over New England, throwing just one pass the entire game. That same season, I believe, he also engaged in a classic shootout with Joe Namath, throwing nearly every down and nearly winning a high-scoring, back-and-forth affair. It's often said that competitors like Unitas never lose, they just run out of time.

"Just in the past year I was sitting at a University of Maryland basketball game, on press row, just a few feet behind Unitas' courtside seat," Ashley recalled. "He had become a fixture at major sporting events in Maryland in his last few years. Unitas loved rooting for hometown heroes—certainly he recognized greatness.

"I did too. I've interviewed big-time coaches and athletes for 20 years now, but I never could get up the courage to say something to Johnny U that night. I wanted to tell him what he meant to my brother and—by association—to me. But I couldn't quite find the words. So I just nodded at him as he walked by and he flashed a smile just before he was engulfed by others who felt comfortable talking up a legend."

Chapter 2

The Long Shot Pays Off

"He was one of the toughest competitors I ever knew, and overcame tremendous odds to become one of the greatest players in NFL history." —Don Shula

Fans and sportswriters alike recall the two great drives that Johnny Unitas engineered to will the Baltimore Colts to overtime victory in the 1958 NFL Championship Game. What many don't recall is that on his first great drive to tie the game and send it into overtime, Unitas connected on only one of his first five passes.

That drive in itself was emblematic of Unitas' long, difficult road to the top. His life story should be required reading for any young athlete who thinks that the very best are identified by the experts at a young age. The very best are identified only by their will to make themselves the best over many years.

"He was one of the toughest competitors I ever knew, and overcame tremendous odds to become one of the greatest players in NFL history," said Don Shula, his coach from 1963 to 1969.

Those tremendous odds began on May 7, 1933, when Unitas was born in Pittsburgh, Pennsylvania, to a family of Lithuanian origins. Five years later the odds grew much worse when his father died, leaving a widow and four children under age 10. Their primary inheritance? A failing coal-delivery business.

To keep food on the table his mother took coal orders all day long, then went to her job as a scrubwoman in downtown office buildings. Later she returned to school, completed bookkeeping training, and worked as a bookkeeper for the city of Pittsburgh for many years. The example Mrs. Unitas set left her son with an unflappability, a calm in the face of big pressure.

"It was too much for her," Unitas once recalled. "The business failed. But we never missed a meal. She was marvelous."

As a little guy Johnny helped the family by shoveling coal around the neighborhood for 75 cents a ton. As soon as he was old enough he got his working papers and joined a construction crew. But education remained a priority, no matter how hard he worked to help the family.

He was a slender halfback for St. Justin's, a small Catholic school in Pittsburgh. He moved to quarterback in his senior year, weighing in at a miniscule 145 pounds. He was 6' tall and good enough to earn All-Catholic honors in the city.

His big hope was to get a scholarship to Notre Dame. The St. Justin's coaches managed to get him an invitation to visit the South Bend campus, but the coaches there got one look at his frame and sent back a note to his school. "The boy is too light," it said.

Disheartened but still determined, Unitas began contacting college teams himself. There seemed to be little interest, meaning he might be destined—like others his age—for a life in the local steel mills. Then the University of Louisville responded to his inquiry, liked what they saw, and offered him a scholarship.

In those days freshmen were eligible and Unitas

He was on the third string and sure that the coaches were planning to cut him. But somehow he got on the field and completed 11 of his first 12 passes.

quickly found his career threatened before it got started. He was on the third string and sure that the coaches were planning to cut him. But somehow he got on the field against St. Bonaventure and completed 11 of his first 12 passes on his way to throwing for more than 300 yards and three touchdowns.

"He was a little kid, skinny, with that same crew cut that he has today," Louisville coach Frank Camp later recalled. "He was shy off the field, but once he went out there to play he was the boss."

One of the key moments of his early college career came in the fourth quarter against the University of Houston. The score was tied at 21–21 with time running down and Louisville in possession of the ball on Houston's 40. On third-and-two the Cardinals' fullback demanded, "Give me the ball. I'll get the two yards."

"When I want you to take the ball," Unitas shot back, "I'll tell you." He then called a pass play and nailed the throw for the winning touchdown.

Then there was the 59–6 pounding at the hands of the University of Tennessee during which Unitas was sacked repeatedly. His determination in the pocket that day prompted Tennessee coach Bowden Wyatt to call Unitas "the best quarterback I've seen this year."

By his senior year he had matured into a 190-pounder with the toughness and skills to get the attention of pro scouts. He suffered a hairline fracture of his ankle but refused to miss more than one game that season.

His hometown Steelers took him in the ninth round of the 1955 NFL draft, but their top quarterback was Jim Finks. Also ahead of Unitas on the depth charts were Ted Marchibroda and Vic Eaton.

Unitas looked good in camp scrimmages, throwing for two touchdowns and breaking a run for 25 yards, but coach Walt Keisling never inserted him into any of the team's preseason games. Then the Steelers waited until just before the start of the regular season to cut him, too late for him to catch on with another team.

Keisling gave him $10 and told him to head home. "I wouldn't mind," Unitas told the coach, "but I never got a chance to play."

He was 22 with a pregnant wife, Dorothy, who was living with her parents. To save money he pocketed the $10 and hitchhiked home, where he picked up work on a pile-driving crew. Soon he was climbing oil rigs for grease jobs.

To keep his football dreams alive he took up playing for $3 a game under Pennsylvania's old Bloomfield Bridge on a roster loaded with steel-mill workers, many of them disabled. The offensive line alone featured just seven arms.

"The oil-soaked Bloomfield Bridge," he once told sportswriter Paul Zimmerman. "The Bloomfield Rams. I was in the infant stage. Still learning. Chuck Rogers, the guy who owned the team, was the quarterback. I had to battle him for the job. We had two fullbacks, Jacko Cray and Red Salender. One was a heavy-equipment driver and the other one was a bartender. We had a 5'6" middle linebacker named Fred Zangara, a Nick Buoniconti type. He could play. Lots of those guys could play."

They could not, however, see much sense in Unitas' continued fantasy that he could star in the NFL.

Upon his release from the Steelers, Unitas had sent a telegram to Paul Brown of the Cleveland Browns. The coach replied that too much of training camp had gone by for the quarterback to be a factor in 1955, but that he would be welcome for training camp the next year.

With hope squarely alive Unitas set about competing in a league where games were played on dimly lit dirt fields and the crowds often struggled to reach triple figures. "Sure, he was the best ballplayer in our league, and everyone knew it," one of his teammates once recalled. "But it still didn't make any sense for a guy playing sandlot ball to be talking about signing with the Cleveland Browns. Guys would needle him. 'Hey,' some guy would yell, 'did you hear about me, Unitas? The Los Angeles Rams want me.' But it didn't bother Johnny any. He kept his mouth shut and played the game. You had to admire him."

He never made that tryout with the Browns. In the spring of the next year, Colts coach Weeb Ewbank invited him to Baltimore for a tryout. Years later a story would surface that a fan had written the Colts suggesting that there was a quarterback with the Bloomfield Rams that they should take a look at.

A packed Memorial Stadium in Baltimore at the outset of the Unitas era.

"I always accuse Johnny of writing that letter," Ewbank would quip whenever he was asked about Unitas' discovery.

Ewbank and the Colts coaches liked what they saw in that tryout and signed him for $7,000. Unitas impressed Ewbank early in the 1956 season with his drive to learn. The schedule opened with the rookie listed as number two on the depth charts behind George Shaw, who had been named the NFL Rookie of the Year a season earlier.

In the fourth game of the season, against the Bears, Shaw went down with a knee injury that sidelined him for the season and shortened his promising career. Suddenly Unitas had his chance, with his team holding a 21–20 lead.

"Get in there and pretend it's just another practice session," Ewbank told him. Unitas saw his first pass intercepted by J. C. Caroline, who ran it back 59 yards for a touchdown. (It would be Caroline that Unitas would burn in 1960 in a last-second victory over Chicago.)

Unitas fumbled three times that day and saw the Bears cover all three on their way to a 58–27 win. In the late moments he threw his first touchdown pass, a 36-yarder to Jim Mutscheller. It was the beginning of his amazing streak of 47 straight games with a touchdown pass—a streak that would run through four seasons.

After that disastrous beginning, Unitas calmly went to Ewbank and told him, "If you give me a chance, I'll show what I can do." Ewbank listened, and it helped save his job.

The Colts came down to the wire on the 1956 season, battling to stay out of last place. In the last game against the Redskins, Baltimore had the ball on its own 47, trailing 17–12 with 15 seconds left. Unitas launched a bomb aimed for Mutscheller. The ball bounced off a receiver into Mutscheller's waiting hands, good enough for the win that saved Ewbank's job and showed that Unitas had no problem being both good and lucky.

In 1957 Unitas completed 57.1 percent of his passes and led the league in yardage with 2,550 yards and 24 touchdowns. The Colts posted a 7–5 record, the first time they had ever posted a winning season in the NFL.

One key moment that season found the Colts facing a third-and-inches at their own 40 against the San Francisco 49ers. Ewbank called for a dive play to fullback Alan Ameche. Unitas instead checked off at the line of scrimmage when he saw the Niner defense stacked for the run and calmly nailed a 15 yarder to Lenny Moore.

Unitas pushed Baltimore to five straight wins to open the 1958 schedule. In the sixth game, against Green Bay, he sustained three broken ribs and suffered a punctured lung. True to form, he only missed two games.

To get him back into action the team had Unitas fitted with an aluminum corset to protect his ribs. Yes, the whole procedure was quite unusual. But Unitas wanted to get back to work.

He had spent his two weeks out of action thinking about the hard road he had traveled to get to this point. Now he had a team that could compete for a championship, and he wanted to be there to lead it. He had this thing about unfinished business.

Chapter 3

The Stuff of Legends

It was the excitement of Johnny Unitas' performance in that 1958 championship game that made clear just how entertaining NFL football could be.

The New York Giants appeared destined for greatness when they bested the run-oriented Cleveland Browns 10–0 in the 1958 playoffs. Folks figured the New Yorkers had the NFL championship as good as won. What followed, though, was history—the kind that soon made people across the country sit up and take notice of pro football.

The 1958 title game was the league's very first sudden-death overtime championship—perfect timing for the first TV broadcast to nail-biting football fans around the world. The game and this young rising star Unitas revealed a new, exciting edge to what many had considered an old game of thuds and thumps.

After years of trying to get the kind of interest and fan following that college football had enjoyed for decades, the pro game was on the cusp of finding a home in the hearts of millions of fans. NBC had paid $100,000 in 1955 to televise the NFL championship, and in the wake of the 1958 championship game it seemed like a sure bet for the networks to begin showing regular-season games.

It was the excitement of Johnny Unitas' performance in that 1958 championship that made clear just how entertaining NFL football could be.

"All of a sudden," said Roone Arledge, the pioneer of sports television at ABC, "the networks woke up and saw that they had to have football."

The cast for the 1958 title game involved many of the league's truly great figures. Tom Landry and Vince Lombardi were assistants to Giant coach Jim Lee Howell. Alex

Webster and Frank Gifford were residents of the New York backfield along with grizzled Charlie Conerly at quarterback. Pat Summerall was the place-kicker.

But that was merely the offensive unit. The rocks in New York's ribs were defenders: Sam Huff and Cliff Livingston at linebacker, Dick Modzelewski and Rosey Grier at tackle, Andy Robustelli at end, Jimmy Patton and Emlen Tunnell in the secondary. Landry was the mind behind the monster, aligning this talent in a 4-3 defense that flexed and crushed opponents, creating a resurgence in New York football that filled the throngs in Yankee Stadium with raving, noisy madness during each home game. "Defense!" the Giants crowd repeatedly roared.

And defense is what Landry gave them. The Giants had given up a league-low 183 points and outlasted Cleveland three times to win the Eastern Conference title.

The Colts? They were led by this nearly anonymous supernova, Unitas. Sure, Johnny U had been named the league MVP in 1957 for his role in making winners of the perennial doormat Colts, but he was still a reasonably well-kept secret by the 1958 title game. Until then no one realized he could work absolute magic.

Nevertheless, Baltimore was anything but a one-man show. Rangy and precise

Raymond Berry was the split end and Unitas' main target. L. G. Dupre and Alan the "Horse" Ameche were the power in the backfield. Lenny Moore was the philly, the flanker/halfback, the game breaker.

> # Johnny U had been named the league MVP in 1957 for making winners of the perennial doormat Colts, but he was still a reasonably well-kept secret by the 1958 title game.

The Colts played a little defense too, with Gino Marchetti at end, Gene "Big Daddy" Lipscomb at tackle, Don Shinnick and Bill Pellington backing the line, and nasty, naughty Johnny Sample in the secondary. Combined, they were team enough for a 9–3 record and the Western Championship over Chicago.

Still, New York had won the regular-season contest between the two teams and Baltimore hadn't beaten the Giants since 1954. Furthermore, the setting for their title showdown was Yankee Stadium, filled with 64,175 noisy New Yorkers lusting for the thud of the Giants defense. A few million more tuned in on television.

What they saw initially didn't seem likely to snare legions of new viewers. The first quarter brought just the slightest taste of offense, as neither team could gain a first down in the opening 10 minutes. Finally New York sustained a drive to the Colts' 36 from where Summerall kicked a field goal.

The Colts finally answered in the second quarter, after Big Daddy Lipscomb recovered a Gifford fumble (he was to lose the ball three times in the quarter) inside the New York 20-yard line. Baltimore hammered into the end zone on a series of dives, with Ameche going the final two yards for a 7–3 lead.

Toward the close of the half the Giants again threatened, but Gifford lost a second fumble, this time inside the Baltimore 15-yard line. The Colts recovered and began another grinding march. Using mostly running plays, Unitas directed the Colts to the New York 15.

From there he zipped a pass to Berry in the end zone. With a 14–3 halftime advantage, the Colts were able to take some of the zeal out of the home crowd. The numbness deepened in the third quarter as Baltimore drove to the Giants' 3-yard line, where Landry's unit dug in.

For three downs the defense held. On fourth down Colts coach Weeb Ewbank opted against a field goal and went for six points. The Giants repelled Ameche and started their comeback.

"We talked about [a field goal]," Ewbank told reporters afterward. "But I wanted to bury them right there with a touchdown."

Instead, the Giants found the necessary momentum. Two running plays moved the ball to the 13, where Conerly threw deep to veteran receiver Kyle Rote. Caught from behind at the Colt 25, Rote fumbled. Webster, who was trailing the play, scooped up the ball and advanced it to the Baltimore 1.

On the next play Mel Triplett punched in for the score. After Summerall's conversion the Giants had closed to 14–10, and the crowd had regained its lustiness.

Landry's defense did its job throughout the remainder of the period, and the fourth quarter opened with the Giants driving for the go-ahead score. With less than a minute gone in the period Gifford caught a 15-yard touchdown pass, and New York regained the lead, 17–14.

The descending late-afternoon darkness couldn't have been more figurative for the Colts. The stadium lights were turned on as Baltimore set up to receive the kickoff.

In the early going of the fourth Landry's unit prevailed, dousing two Colts drives and giving the offense the opportunity to control the ball and the game with a late drive to eat the clock. Facing a third-and-four at the New York 40, Conerly called for Gifford to power off tackle. Gifford, better known in his sports afterlife as an ABC-TV broadcaster, would swear for years afterward that he made it. Marchetti, Shinnick, and Lipscomb were the stoppers for Baltimore.

Gifford seemed to nudge past the first-down marker, but veteran head linesman Charley Berry and referee Ron Gibbs assessed the forward progress and moved the ball back to where they saw Gifford downed. When the pile was untangled, Marchetti was carried from the field with a fractured leg, and New York was inches short of the first down. The crowd, of course, howled otherwise.

"We only needed four inches," Giants lineman Jack Stroud said in *The Game of Their Lives*. "We would have run through a brick wall at that point."

Howell figured he had little choice but to punt, and Giants kicker Don Chandler responded with a beauty, pinning the Colts at their 14 with 1:56 left. "I was sure then it was all over," Lombardi said afterward.

But Unitas found a spark and turned it into a flame. After two dud plays the Colts faced third-and-10. Unitas answered with a toss to Moore for a first down at the 25. In

Defensive end Gino Marchetti was one of the Colts' heroes of the 1958 title game in New York.

the mix of ensuing plays came three brilliant completions to Berry: first a slant up the middle for 25 yards, followed by a diving reception at the 35, and finished by a quick hook at the 13.

"John knew where to attack the defense," Giants linebacker Huff would later allow ruefully. "He found a weakness and exploited it to perfection. 'Unitas to Berry, Unitas to Berry, Unitas to Berry.' It still rings in my ears."

With 0:07 left, Colts kicker Steve Myhra calmly entered the game and tied the score at 17. The numbness again descended on the New York crowd. This sudden-death overtime stuff was new territory, even in the Big Apple.

"We were so damn disgusted with ourselves that when we got the ball for that last series, we struck back at the Giants in a sort of blind fury," Unitas said afterward of the drive to tie the game.

His magic, however, drooped briefly as he made the wrong call on the coin toss for overtime. "When we tied the game," he said later, "we were all standing around scratching our heads, waiting for someone to make a decision what to do. . . . They sent me out for the flip of the coin. All they told me was, 'Get the ball if you can.' "

The Giants won the toss and elected to receive.

"We were standing around saying, 'If we get John the ball, we're going to win the game,'" Colts defensive tackle Art Donovan recalled. "It was that simple."

Simple worked well enough. After three plays the Giants still needed a yard for a first down, so Chandler again punted beautifully. The Colts took over on their 20 and Unitas started them down the field into history.

To minimize the chances of a turnover, Unitas kept the ball on the ground. Dupre ran for 11 yards, then after two failed dives Unitas gambled and shot a flare pass to Ameche in the flats, and the Horse bulled to another first down.

The progress was halted momentarily when Modzelewski lanced through the heart of the pocket and sacked Unitas for an eight-yard loss. Looking at third-and-long, Unitas executed what the analysts came to savor as the game's most crucial play. First he dropped to pass, hesitated, then broke to the left seemingly headed for the end, stopped, faked a pass, then faded farther out. Berry, shaking and darting, broke open when Giants halfback Carl Karilivacz stumbled. Still, Unitas hesitated, motioning for Berry to go farther. Finally satisfied, he zipped the ball 21 yards to Berry's wide target, No. 82, for another first down at the New York 42.

The unsung heroes of that great moment were the Colts' offensive linemen—George Preas and company—who kept Unitas free for a leisurely scramble.

With the Giants ripe for the fall, Unitas called the draw to Ameche. It went for 22 yards and another first down just inside the Giants' 20. The New York defense tightened and stopped a run for a one-yard gain. But Unitas followed that with a throw to Berry at the 8.

On the verge of one of football's greatest moments, with nearly everyone in Yankee Stadium sensing an imminent field goal, a fan broke loose from the crowd and headed onto the field. Play was stopped for a full minute until police could entice him back into the stands. Unitas watched calmly, then crossed up the defense again when play resumed, throwing a sideline pass to tight end Jim Mutscheller, who went out of bounds at the 1-yard line.

The next call was a dive to Ameche. The hole was wide, to say the least, and instead of defenders the Horse was greeted by joyous Baltimore fans who rushed the end zone to greet him.

"When I slapped the ball into Ameche's belly and saw him take off," Unitas told reporters, "I knew nobody was gonna stop him."

The fans wrested away the game ball, and several Colts chased them down to retrieve it. Unitas had completed 26 of 40 passes for 349 yards. Berry had caught 12 for 178 yards. The Giants had set a dubious record with six fumbles. Soon after the roar grew to a din, the Colts retired to the locker room to savor their winners' checks: $4,718.77 apiece.

"The guys made the plays; I was more of a catalyst," Unitas would say years later when asked about his role in football's pivotal game. "I just called the plays. They did the work. I just had to stand back there and direct them."

Berry disagreed: "He was the difference in the game. The two-minute drive to tie

> **"The guys made the plays; I was more of a catalyst," Unitas said of his role in football's pivotal game. "They did the work. I just had to stand back there and direct them."**

the game—that is my highest memory of my entire pro playing career."

"That game was the highlight of my entire pro career," Berry offered again four decades later. "When John was out here this summer, I asked him, 'Why did you come to me three times in a row?' He looked at me and said, 'I figured you would catch it.' "

The game had been blacked out on television in New York but shown everywhere else by NBC. In Baltimore a loose cable knocked the game off the air during the overtime. TV screens went blank for 2 1/2 minutes during the Colts' final drive, but a timeout gave the network time enough to get it fixed so that Baltimore viewers could see Ameche's score.

"The drama came from the championship setting, rather than the game itself, until we came down to tie it in the final seconds. And then it became the first playoff ever to go to sudden death, and you can't have much more drama than that," Unitas recalled.

In the excitement of the aftermath NFL commissioner Bert Bell declared the contest the "Greatest Game Ever Played," a description that would be repeated again and again over the following decades.

Great changes lay ahead for pro football, which had suddenly become a hot TV property. Sadly, Commissioner Bell died of a heart attack in October while watching his beloved Eagles and Steelers play, but his eventual replacement was a bright young PR executive named Pete Rozelle, who would guide the game to greater heights.

Yet for those who saw him perform, for those who played with and against him, it was obvious that the heart of the game's new popularity was the charisma of Johnny Unitas.

"It gets clearer every year," Berry explained years later. "To be able to be in Baltimore as a receiver and get to play 12 years with him, I have to classify as the best break I ever got in my career. The type of quarterback he was, the leader he was, he was totally focused on moving the football, scoring points, and winning. He never thought about records and individual things; he was all business. He was the toughest competitor you could hope for."

Colts fullback Ameche advances through a big opening to score the winning touchdown in overtime against the New York Giants at Yankee Stadium in New York on December 28, 1958.

Chapter 4

A Reign of Dominance

"He'd get knocked down play after play, yet he'd be right up there where the ref put the ball down, checking the clock and knowing how much yardage he needed." —Buddy Young

Halfback/defensive back Alex Hawkins recalled some years after the fact that "From the moment Alan Ameche scored in overtime against the Giants in 1958, the city of Baltimore belonged to the Colts."

And the Colts?

Well, they belonged to John Unitas. His teammates universally loved him, would do anything for him, recalled running back Buddy Young. "You know what convinced me?" Young said. "He'd get knocked on his fanny play after play, yet he'd be right up there at the spot where the referee was putting the ball down, and then he'd be checking the clock and knowing how much yardage he needed."

They were a rough-and-tumble lot of veterans, but that continuing display of courage sealed the deal for the Colts. Likewise for the city and the entire region.

Everybody loved Johnny.

Baltimore was the country's eighth largest city in those days and had possessed this latest version of the Colts (there had been an earlier version in the All-America Football Conference that had failed after joining the NFL) for less than a decade. It was strictly a blue-collar town, featuring street after street of row houses and neighborhood bars.

That helps explain why it didn't take long for the city to tie its image to the upstart football team and its quarterback. With his winning ways Unitas offered the opportunity for the city to boost its self-esteem. He might have become the Emperor of Baltimore if he had been so inclined. His social life, though, extended only to a quick beer with his

This 13-yard pass to Raymond Berry against Washington on September 25, 1960, ran Unitas' league touchdown pass record to 38 consecutive games.

teammates after a hard day's work. From there he headed home to the wife and kids.

Whatever the Unitas appeal, it certainly didn't stem from his looks, according to Hawkins, who wrote in his autobiography *My Story* that Unitas "looked so much like a Mississippi farm hand that I looked around for a mule. He had stooped shoulders, a chicken breast, thin, bowed legs, and long, dangling arms with crooked, mangled fingers fastened to a pair of very large hands."

"He was a big boy, with good speed," Colts coach Weeb Ewbank said. "Not dazzling speed, but good speed. And he was so very eager to learn."

That eagerness meant that he had come very quickly to master the game. In fact he had reduced it to something of a science, especially when it came to finding favorite receiver Raymond Berry. "It takes me 1.2 seconds to retreat seven yards behind the line of scrimmage," he explained. "A quarterback should need protection for 2.5 seconds, so now I've got 1.3 seconds to get rid of the ball. Then, if it's not too long a pass, the ball's in flight for one second. It should be in Raymond's hands at 3.5. If it isn't, we're not throwing the right distance for that particular play."

The league's players had voted him the Most Valuable Player for the second straight year in 1958. Despite his youth he always presented the image of a forceful, confident leader. "Anything I do," he said, "I always have a reason for."

> **"He was a big boy, with good speed. Not dazzling speed, but good speed. And he was so very eager to learn."**
>
> —Weeb Ewbank

Those large hands threw for 32 touchdowns in 1959, a mastery matched only by the running brilliance of Cleveland Browns halfback Jim Brown, who was in the process of rolling through a string of rushing titles. Led by their young stars, the Colts and the Browns always seemed to stage epic battles for nothing more than a day's bragging rights.

November 1, 1959, brought yet another of those Colts/Browns clashes. Brown was magnificent, piling up 176 yards and five touchdowns. "One of the greatest performances ever," according to Cleveland coach Paul Brown.

For his part, Unitas did nothing to hurt his own growing legend. He passed for 397 yards and four touchdowns. It just wasn't enough to offset Brown, as Cleveland won 38–31.

As the clock wound down the fans in Baltimore gave Brown a standing ovation. The Browns, though, were too far behind in the standings. It was the Colts that were again headed to the playoffs, where they would make their way to a rematch with the Giants in the NFL Championship Game.

The Giants led 9–7 on three Pat Summerall field goals until the Colts erupted for three touchdowns in the fourth period. The killer score was Johnny Sample's 42-yard return of an interception. In addition, Unitas used his chicken legs to run for the go-ahead touchdown.

He then passed for a fourth-quarter score that extended Baltimore's lead to 21–9. They would go on to win 31–16. Unitas had done it again, completing 18 of 29 passes for 265 yards and two touchdowns.

"The most important thing of all about Unitas," said Ewbank, "is that he had a real hunger. This was a kid who wanted success and didn't have it so long that he wasn't about to waste it when it came."

Where had this greatness come from? Unitas himself attributed it to an older uncle who often cared for the kids while their mom worked at one of her many jobs.

"My uncle encouraged me to play football," he once recalled. "He liked to catch a ball with me. I certainly never thought I could even play for my high school team. I was always the smallest boy in my class."

Was this the same recruit that Notre Dame passed over because of his size? Was this the kid who couldn't pass the entrance exam for the University of Pittsburgh? Was this the same player the Pittsburgh Steelers had figured wasn't smart enough to direct an NFL offense?

The numbers seemed to suggest that maybe it was someone else, that there had been a mistake. His numbers were phenomenal: two league championships, two league MVPs, and that growing string of consecutive games with a touchdown pass.

Circumstances should have indicated that his record, which had grown to rival the consecutive-game hitting streak of Joe DiMaggio, would be in trouble with the coming of the 1960 season. Unitas himself was just heading into his prime, but the Colts roster of veterans had begun to show its age. Looming in the team's rearview mirror was the young, talented Green Bay squad assembled by coach Vince Lombardi.

Unitas' streak had run to 47 games when the Colts went to L.A. Coliseum to face the Rams and their vaunted defense. Down 10–3 late in the fourth period, Unitas drove his team to the Rams' 12-yard line. But there the Colts stalled on third down.

Facing fourth down with less than 90 seconds to go, Unitas called for a corner route to his prime target, Berry. True to the plan, Berry broke open at the right time and Unitas made the throw.

"I never had to see Ray for more than a split second," Unitas explained later. "I always knew exactly where he would be. After all those years we could read every move the other made."

But this time Berry's bad leg gave out on his way to the corner of the end zone. He fell, and Unitas' pass fell incomplete. The streak that had lasted four and a half seasons was over.

"The last thing I remember about the play," Unitas told reporters, "was Ray pounding the ground with his fist."

Unitas smiled about the circumstances, but the situation for the Colts themselves was no laughing matter. On the day that he burned the Bears for that come-from-behind victory at Wrigley Field, the Colts pushed their record to 6–2. But the next week Alan Ameche tore his Achilles tendon in a last-second loss to Detroit, and the Colts never won another game that season, finishing 6–6.

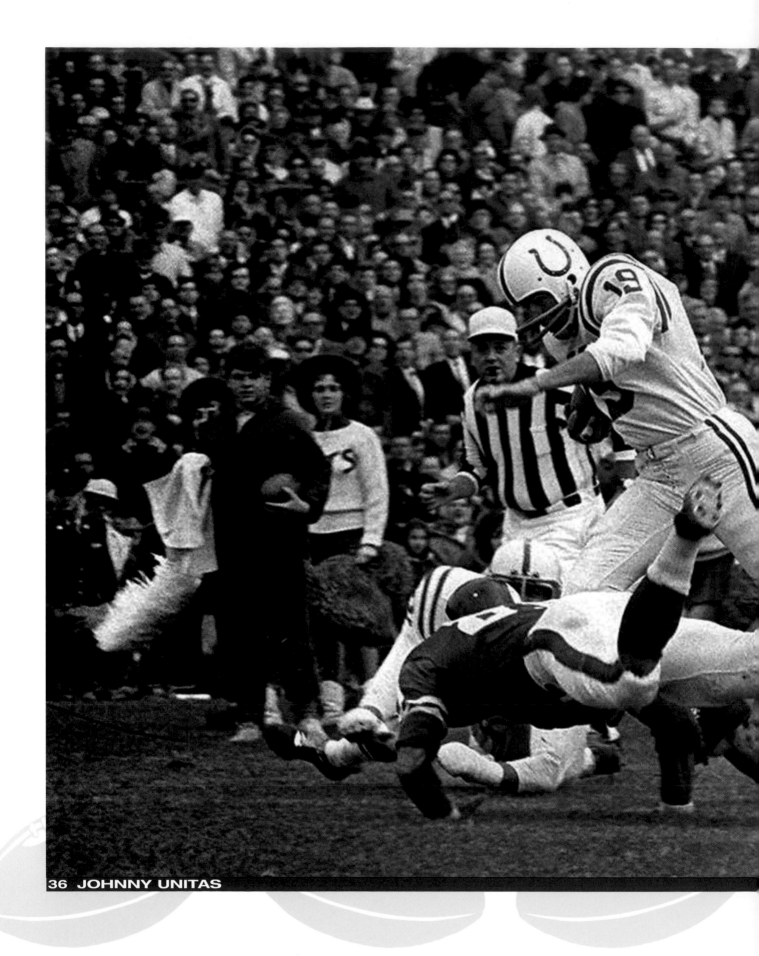

In 1961 a dislocated middle finger left Unitas struggling to grip the ball. In 1962 the once prolific Colts offense went seven straight quarters without scoring a TD. After the 1962 campaign Ewbank was fired and replaced by Don Shula. A former defensive back with the Colts, Shula quickly put the team back on a winning track behind young stars such as Tom Matte and John Mackey.

Unitas regained his form in 1963. His 3,481 yards passing was the best in the NFL. And in 1964 he earned his third league MVP when he led Baltimore to a 12-2 record. He also ranked first in the league in yards per pass attempt (9.26).

Lenny Moore also had a fine season that year, leading the league in rushing touchdowns. Baltimore scored a club-record 428 points and led the NFL in both scoring offense and defense, but they were upset by Cleveland 27-0 in the NFL Championship Game.

The 1965 season found Unitas and backup QB Gary Cuozzo sidelined by injury. The Colts, though, prospered when Shula turned the signal calling over to halfback Matte, who had played quarterback at Ohio State.

Baltimore finished with a 10-3-1 record and a tie with Green Bay for the Western Division title. In a playoff in frigid Wisconsin, the Colts lost to the Packers 13-10 in overtime.

The ups and downs continued from there. In 1967 Unitas had a league-high 58.5 completion percentage, but by late in the year he was plagued by a severely sore arm, one that specialists suggested had been strained by his unorthodox throwing motion.

"I think it needs rest," Unitas said.

"It's like a baseball pitcher. When you get a sore arm, you have to stop throwing."

His chronically sore elbow meant that Shula and the Colts had to turn to journeyman Earl Morall for 1968. The veteran enjoyed his finest season, throwing for a league-high 26 touchdowns and winning the league's MVP award as he led the Colts to a 13–1 regular-season record.

That team's strength lay in its punishing defense. Led by All-Pro linebacker Mike Curtis, cornerback Bobby Boyd, and safety Rick Volk, Shula and assistants Bill Arnsparger and Chuck Noll installed a blitzing scheme that shut out three opponents and tied an NFL record by allowing just 144 points.

The Colts routed the Browns 34–0 for the NFL championship and prepared to face the New York Jets in Super Bowl III. Unitas yearned to play in the big game, but Shula understandably gave the starting nod to Morrall.

The Colts were 18- to 23-point favorites. Everyone figured the Baltimore defense would make mincemeat of Super Joe Namath and company—which made Namath's mouthing off to the press in the days before the Super Bowl seem all the more preposterous. "The Jets will win on Sunday," he told the Miami Touchdown Club three days before the game. "I guarantee it."

Unitas regained his form in 1963. His 3,481 yards passing was the best in the NFL. And in 1964 he earned his third league MVP when he led Baltimore to a 12—2 record.

Later he told reporters that Morrall wasn't as good as three or four AFL quarterbacks. Then he was reported to have told Colts defensive end Lou Michaels, "We're going to beat the hell out of you."

The Colts were a little taken aback by the woofing. "All this Namath talk isn't going to fire us up," grumbled Baltimore's Bubba Smith.

The game had additional subplots. Ewbank, who had directed Baltimore to the world championships in 1958 and 1959, only to be let go after the .500 season in 1962, was now the New York coach. And Sample, who had been traded by the Colts after their championships, was the firebrand in the Jets' secondary.

In the days before the big game, club and network (NBC had paid $2.5 million for broadcast rights) officials began planning the victory celebration in the Baltimore locker room. Colts owner Carroll Rosenbloom went so far as to invite Ewbank to his victory party.

The Colts, it's fair to say, played as they acted: flatly overconfident. Still, they were presented ample opportunity in the first half to make the game a blowout. It just wasn't in the stars.

The Colts promptly shoved their way down the field early in the game to a first down at the Jets 19, where a pass was dropped and Lou Michaels missed a 27-yard field goal.

Baltimore's Bubba Smith applies pressure to New York's Joe Namath in Super Bowl III.

Moments later George Sauer fumbled on New York's 12 and the Colts had another chance. Jets defensive back Randy Beverly intercepted a Morrall pass in the end zone.

The Baltimore defense was successful in shutting down Namath's primary target, Don Maynard, so he threw to Sauer instead, moving the Jets on an impressive drive to the Baltimore 4, where Matt Snell ran the ball in for a 7–0 lead.

Again the Colts forged back, taking the ball to the Jets 16 on the strength of a 58-yard run by Matte. And again the Jets prevailed, this time with Sample getting the interception in the end zone.

Still, the Colts returned to scoring position yet a fourth time just before the half; but Morrall failed to see wide-open Jimmy Orr at the Jets' 10. Instead he threw to the other side of the field and suffered a third interception.

The second half opened with the sore-armed Unitas eager to play, but Shula started Morrall again. Then Matte fumbled on the opening play, New York recovered, and increased the lead to 10–0 on a Jim Turner field goal. After Morrall failed to move the team a second time, Shula inserted Unitas.

"I knew I couldn't throw a long pass," Unitas explained afterward. "But I figured we could still score if I could get a short one in the right place."

The Jets, though, had shut down Baltimore's strong ground game and defended the pass ferociously. Meanwhile, Namath was troubled by a thumb injury and replaced by veteran backup Babe Parilli, who promptly took the Jets to another third-quarter field goal and a 13–0 lead.

When Turner kicked yet another field goal two minutes into the fourth quarter for a 16–0 lead, the task for Baltimore and Unitas became nearly impossible. But he pushed the team upfield just like he had in his prime.

With four minutes left, Jerry Hill scored on a one-yard dive and the NFL's dominant team avoided a shutout.

Twice more Unitas and the Colts got the ball back. On one possession he threw an interception. On another they ran out of downs.

Afterward the Jets acknowledged that they were truly scared with the ball in Unitas' hands, never mind his sore arm. When New York gained possession after his final incompletion, the Jets knew it was time to celebrate.

"We had the ball," said New York's Larry Grantham. "For the first time, I knew we had won the ballgame. Nobody could take it away from us. Nobody. Not even the great Johnny Unitas."

Namath and Ewbank celebrate following the Jets' stunning victory over Unitas and the Colts in Super Bowl III.

Chapter 5

Completing the Legacy

It wasn't always pretty, or pleasing to the fans, but he still managed to contribute and even walked away with a Super Bowl ring.

The years of defying defenses had begun to catch up with John Unitas. He spent his last few years in the league unable to make the throws that had once made him so dangerous.

Still, he fought through the elbow pain, trying to compete. It wasn't always pretty, or pleasing to the fans, but he still managed to contribute and even walked away with a Super Bowl ring.

The organization of the NFL/AFL merger was negotiated in 1969, when Baltimore, Cleveland, and Pittsburgh agreed to join the 13-member American Football Conference, which was realigned in Western, Eastern, and Central divisions.

The Colts had been through changes as well, with Don Shula being replaced by tall, quiet Don McCafferty, who had been an assistant, first under Ewbank, then under Shula. The change was not unwelcome to the players.

Where Shula was emotional and, at times, tempestuous in his approach to the game, McCafferty was more relaxed in dealing with his athletes. "Don has a great knowledge of football," Unitas explained. "He is a calm, collected individual. He doesn't shout and scream. He is able to look at football objectively without getting carried away emotionally."

With this refreshing atmosphere the Colts posted an 11–2–1 regular-season record that included a 35–0 victory over Shula's Miami Dolphins.

From there they battled their way to the AFC Championship Game, which was a

matchup of old men: Unitas and the Colts vs. the ancient George Blanda (a backup forced into duty) and the Oakland Raiders. Unitas hit on only 11 of his 30 passing attempts for 245 yards that day, but he clinched the 27–17 victory with a 68-yard scoring pass to Ray Perkins.

With the win the Colts moved on to Miami to face the NFC-champion Dallas Cowboys in Super Bowl V, which has come to hang in the American memory as the "Blooper Bowl" because of its many turnovers and screwups.

In the days before the big game, reporters asked Unitas about the atmosphere and the Colts' chance for redemption after the embarrassing loss to the Jets in Super Bowl III.

"It's just another game," Johnny U replied. "The money makes it different."

Reporters then asked about his aging arm and the booing of fans displeased that he could no longer meet their huge expectations. "I don't care. I can't care," he said. "I don't care what people say and I don't care what you write. All that matters is the team, the game, and winning."

It would prove a good day to tune out the negatives. In Super Bowl V, the Cowboys and the Colts shared 11 turnovers between them.

The Cowboys still

> # Wherever Johnny Unitas went he left admirers in his wake. Just how deep that admiration ran became clear in the wake of his death on September 11, 2002.

managed an early 6–0 lead on a pair of field goals. Then Unitas struck, or something like that. He overthrew receiver Eddie Hinton by 20 yards only to have the ball settle into the hands of trusty old John Mackey, who turned and ran 45 yards for a touchdown. It went in the books as a 75-yard TD pass.

On the next series Unitas fumbled on his own 28 after getting hammered by the Cowboys' Lee Roy Jordan. The Cowboys quickly converted for a 13–7 lead.

On the following series Unitas threw an interception and was replaced by Earl Morrall, whom he had replaced in Super Bowl III against the Jets. Unitas didn't play again that day.

The game is best described as a defensive struggle that rested on Mike Curtis' fourth-quarter interception of Dallas QB Craig Morton's pass. Rookie Baltimore place-kicker Jim O'Brien's 32-yard field goal with five seconds left gave the Colts a 16–13 win.

Unitas finished three of nine for 88 yards, one TD, and two interceptions. It wasn't beautiful, but the victory would do for an old man still trying to compete.

The championship ignited an explosion of pride in Baltimore. Colts fever soared through the next season as Baltimore finished with a 10–4 record and set a club record by allowing only 140 points. But Shula's Dolphins pounded them 21–0 in the AFC title game.

Then, on July 26, 1972, a day that will live in infamy in Baltimore, Robert Irsay, a 49-year-old businessman from Illinois, picked up the franchise from Carroll Rosenbloom in exchange for Irsay's Los Angeles Rams franchise. Irsay would later break hearts in the city by moving the team to Indianapolis, but before that dark day Irsay engineered the departure of the city's longtime hero.

Unitas was traded to the San Diego Chargers on January 22, 1973. He struggled through one more campaign and retired after the 1973 season with 22 NFL records, among them marks for most passes attempted and completed, most yards gained passing, most touchdown passes, and most seasons leading the league in TD passes.

He returned to his home in Baltimore after his playing days were over and spent the better part of three decades soaking in the love of the city. A favorite at sporting events across Maryland, Unitas' understated style befit a man known for his grace and moxie.

No matter how many games he won by making huge last-second plays, he never seemed to erupt into wild celebration, choosing instead to walk off nonchalantly so that he could quietly enjoy a job well done.

Wherever Johnny Unitas went he left admirers in his wake. Just how deep that admiration ran became clear in the wake of his death of a heart attack on September 11, 2002. Many paid tribute to him.

"I've always said the purest definition of leadership was watching Johnny Unitas get off the team bus," said Ernie Accorsi, general manager of the New York Giants, a former Colts executive and a good Unitas friend.

Raymond Berry said Unitas was special because of "his uncanny instinct for calling the right play at the right time, his icy composure under fire, his fierce competitiveness, and his utter disregard for his own safety."

Many heartfelt tributes also came from the University of Louisville, where Unitas played from 1951 to 1954. The Cardinals only won 12 games in those four seasons, but he threw for 2,912 yards and 27 touchdowns.

"I think everyone knows how much Johnny Unitas meant to our university and the city of Louisville," athletic director Tom Jurich told reporters. "His work on the football field is immortalized by a statue in our stadium, but Johnny Unitas the person will be immortalized in our hearts forever."

At the north end zone of Papa John's Cardinal Stadium is a statue of Unitas. Fittingly, he's searching for a receiver, ready to throw.

Another honor is the Johnny Unitas Golden Arm Award given by the Frank Camp Chapter of the Johnny Unitas Golden Arm Educational Foundation. A college quarterback is picked for the award by a panel of experts each year.

"Johnny Unitas was a great football player, a great person, and a true friend," Louisville head coach John L. Smith said. "He is the foundation of our program and his legacy extends far beyond his accomplishments on the football field. He touched so many young people through his foundation and he will never be forgotten."

The same sentiments ran rampant in the NFL upon word of his death.

"Johnny Unitas will always be a legendary name in NFL history," league commissioner Paul Tagliabue said. "One of the greatest quarterbacks to ever play the game, he epitomized the position with his leadership skills and his ability to perform under pressure."

Among those saddened by his passing was Indianapolis Colts owner Jim Irsay, son of the man who moved the team from Baltimore. "He was a hero to so many people, including me. Over time he became larger than life," Irsay said. "Without question, Johnny was the reason football catapulted to the top of the professional sports world.

"He was a leader in so many ways, a man of indescribable talent and extraordinary character. Johnny leaves us with many great memories from professional football, and we are all grateful for what he gave us in his lifetime."

What would Unitas himself say about all the uproar? Maybe the best answer would be his comment upon being inducted into the Hall of Fame in 1979. "A man never gets to this station in life without being helped, aided, shoved, pushed, and prodded to do better," he said in Canton that day. "I want to be honest with you. The players I played with and the coaches I had . . . they are directly responsible for my being here. I want you all to remember that. I always will."

During his playing days Unitas was sometimes criticized for his seeming arrogance. But he maintained that it was merely confidence based in a belief in his team. "There's a big difference between confidence and conceit," he said. "To me conceit is bragging about yourself. Being confident means you believe you can get the job done, but you know you can't get your job done unless you also have confidence that the other guys are going to get their jobs done too. Without them, I'm nothing."

Career Statistics

Year	Team	G	Comp	Att	Pct	Yds	YPA	TD	Int
1956	Colts	12	110	198	55.6	1,498	7.6	9	10
1957	Colts	12	172	301	57.1	2,550	8.5	24	17
1958	Colts	10	136	263	51.7	2,007	7.6	19	7
1959	Colts	12	193	367	52.6	2,899	7.9	32	14
1960	Colts	12	190	378	50.3	3,099	8.2	25	24
1961	Colts	14	229	420	54.5	2,990	7.1	16	24
1962	Colts	14	222	389	57.1	2,967	7.6	23	23
1963	Colts	14	237	410	57.8	3,481	8.5	20	12
1964	Colts	14	158	305	51.8	2,824	9.3	19	6
1965	Colts	11	164	282	58.2	2,530	9.0	23	12
1966	Colts	14	195	348	56.0	2,748	7.9	22	24
1967	Colts	14	255	436	58.5	3,428	7.9	20	16
1968	Colts	5	11	32	34.4	139	4.3	2	4
1969	Colts	13	178	327	54.4	2,342	7.2	12	20
1970	Colts	14	166	321	51.7	2,213	6.9	14	18
1971	Colts	13	92	176	52.3	942	5.4	3	9
1972	Colts	8	88	157	56.1	1,111	7.1	4	6
1973	Chargers	5	34	76	44.7	471	6.2	3	7
TOTALS		**211**	**2,830**	**5,186**	**54.6**	**40,239**	**7.8**	**290**	**253**